WILD NATURE

AMAZING SHARKS

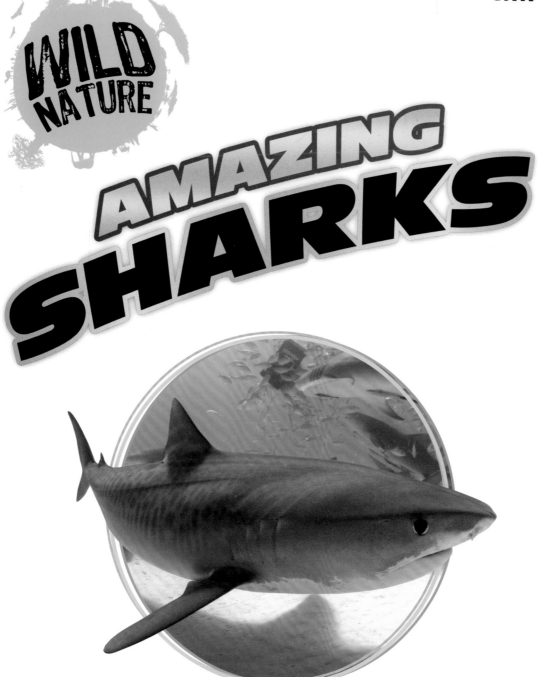

Steve Parker

Miles Kelly

First published as *My Top 20 Sharks* in 2010 by Miles Kelly Publishing Ltd
Harding's Barn, Bardfield End Green, Thaxted, Essex, CM6 3PX, UK

This edition published in 2013

10 9 8 7 6 5 4 3 2 1

Publishing Director Belinda Gallagher
Creative Director Jo Cowan
Editorial Director Rosie McGuire
Senior Editor Claire Philip
Concept Designer Simon Lee
Designers Joe Jones, Rob Hale
Image Manager Liberty Newton
Production Manager Elizabeth Collins
Reprographics Stephan Davis,
Jennifer Hunt, Thom Allaway

ISBN 978-1-78209-095-3

Printed in China

British Library Cataloguing-in-Publication Data
A catalogue record for this book is available from the British Library

ACKNOWLEDGEMENTS
The publishers would like to thank the following sources for the use of their photographs:
Key: (m) = main (i) = inset

Front cover: (main) Mike Parry/Minden Pictures/FLPA, (Wild Nature animal globe) ranker/Shutterstock.com
Back cover: (top) Specta/Shutterstock.com, (bottom) Brandelet/Shutterstock.com
Page 1 A Cotton Photo/Shutterstock.com
Pages 4–5 (clockwise from bottom left) Design Pics Inc/Photolibrary.com, Fred Bavendam/Minden Pictures/FLPA,
Chris and Monique Fallows/Photolibrary.com, Tobias Bernhard/Photolibrary.com, Dan Burton/naturepl.com
Basking shark (m) Dan Burton/naturepl.com, (i) Chris Gomersall/naturepl.com
Blue shark (m) Tobias Bernhard/Photolibrary.com, (i) Richard Herrmann/Photolibrary.com
Great white shark (m) Mike Parry/Minden Pictures/FLPA, (i) Tony Heald/naturepl.com
Greenland shark (m) Doug Perrine/naturepl.com, (i) Doug Perrine/naturepl.com
Bull shark (m) Brandon Cole/naturepl.com, (i) Brandon Cole/naturepl.com
Spiny dogfish (m) Seapics.com
Pacific angel shark (m) Flip Nicklin/Minden Pictures/FLPA
Scalloped hammerhead shark (m) Doug Perrine/naturepl.com, (i) Chris Newbert/Minden Pictures/FLPA
Lemon shark (m) Jeff Rotman/naturepl.com, (i) Brandon Cole/naturepl.com
Leopard shark (m) R.Dirscherl/FLPA, (i) Jurgen Freund/naturepl.com
Megamouth shark (m) Bruce Rasner/Rotman/naturepl.com, (i) Seapics.com
Sand tiger shark (m) Doug Perrine/naturepl.com, (i) Norbert Wu/Minden Pictures/FLPA
Whitetip reef shark (m) Norbert Wu/Minden Pictures/FLPA
Bamboo shark (m) Doug Perrine/naturepl.com
Port Jackson shark (m) Fred Bavendam/Minden Pictures/FLPA, (i) Fred Bavendam/Minden Pictures/FLPA
Swell shark (m) Norbert Wu/Minden Pictures/FLPA, (i) Flip Nicklin/Minden Pictures/FLPA
Tiger shark (m) Norbert Wu/Minden Pictures/FLPA, (i) Michael Pitts/naturepl.com
Whale shark (m) James Watt/Photolibrary.com, (i) Flip Nicklin/Minden Pictures/FLPA
Spotted wobbegong (m) Fred Bavendam/Minden Pictures/FLPA, (i) Chris Newbert/Minden Pictures/FLPA
Shortfin mako (m) Chris and Monique Fallows/Photolibrary.com

Every effort has been made to acknowledge the source and copyright holder of each picture.
Miles Kelly Publishing apologises for any unintentional errors or omissions.

Made with paper from a sustainable forest

www.mileskelly.net   info@mileskelly.net

www.factsforprojects.com

CONTENTS

OUT OF THE BLUE: ULTIMATE KILLERS

Sharks are super predators. Fast and fierce, they can detect prey over great distances. They race in and bite with great power, their razor teeth slicing through flesh, gristle and bone.

Not all sharks are so deadly. The largest of the 400-plus kinds are as big as a bus, yet these giants spend their time filtering tiny planktonic creatures from the sea water. Even the most fearsome predatory sharks rarely attack humans. Road accidents and wasp stings kill more people than shark attacks.

↓ You could easily fit into a basking shark's mouth. But this gentle giant would spit you out – you don't taste like plankton.

↘ Tiger sharks follow a scent trail, their scent-detecting pits picking up the faintest trace of blood from a wounded whale.

SUPER SNOUT

1

ON THE TRAIL

A shark's best long-distance sense is smell. It can detect just a few drops of blood or body fluid floating in the water from hundreds of metres away. It then swims in a zig-zag route, heading to where the smell is strongest.

→ Rushing up from below, a great white's attack carries it clear of the surface, jaws clamped onto its seal victim.

2 ZERO IN

As the shark gets near its potential victim, it takes a good look using its sharp eyesight. A strip of sensors along each side of its body, the lateral line, senses the ripples and currents made by the prey's every move.

BEADY STARE

TIME TO ATTACK!

4 FAST FOOD

The shark charges in for a massively powerful, very fast bite. Then it might back off to see what happens. Usually the victim is badly wounded, so the shark moves in for the kill, and its first mouthful of the meal.

↖ The blue shark swims past possible prey several times, peering closely to judge whether an attack is worth the effort.

↙ A grey reef shark prepares to turn suddenly and dash into the shoal of fish behind, catching some by surprise.

3 FINAL CHARGE

The shark gets within range and senses tiny natural electrical signals made by the active muscles of its target. It may even bump the prey with its nose and nip with its teeth for a quick feel and taste. Finally...

GET READY

Its habit of lazily cruising through the water, sometimes rolling onto its side as though soaking up the sunshine, gave the basking shark its name. This giant – the world's second-largest fish – is far from fierce. As it swims through a shoal of plankton (microscopic creatures that drift in ocean currents), its gaping mouth is one metre wide and one metre high. Water passes into the mouth and out through the gaps between the frilly gill rakers on the sides of the head. Plankton sticks to the rakers and is then sucked down into the shark's stomach.

LAZY BATHER

WE CAN SEE YOU...

The basking shark's tall, triangular fin often pokes above the water's surface as it feeds.

'STAR FACT

Up to one-quarter of a basking shark's weight is its massive liver. This stores food and also contains vast amounts of oils, which are lighter than water and help the shark to float.

SPECIAL FEATURES

SPEED: A basking shark usually swims at a speed slightly slower than we walk. But it can also surge at high speed and even leap clear of the water.

FINS: Its massive front pair of fins (pectorals), give a huge area for control in the water, so this shark can twist and turn surprisingly fast.

GAPE...

The gill rakers look like curving dark stripes inside the shark's mouth. As well as gathering food, they also take in oxygen from the water, allowing the shark to breathe.

Basking shark

Scientific name: *Cetorhinus maximus*
Shark group: Cetorhinidae
Lifespan: Probably 50-plus years
Length: 8–10 m, rarely exceeds 12 m
Weight: Up to 6 tonnes
Range: Oceans worldwide
Status: Vulnerable

RAKERS: The plankton-sieving gill rakers nearly join at the top and bottom, forming an almost complete circle around the shark's head.

JAWS: No other shark can gape at such a wide angle as the basking shark, which swims along with its bendy top and bottom jaws stretched to their limit.

Blue sharks have a habit of following fishing boats in packs, feeding hungrily on discarded scraps thrown overboard. When whaling (whale hunting) was common, they were known for tearing apart whales that were being towed by whaling ships, so sailors called them 'wolves of the sea'. Slim, sleek and speedy, the blue shark can dart and dodge as it chases many kinds of prey, such as fish, squid, crabs and even young dolphins or porpoises.

UNDERWATER WOLVES

ATTACK...

Once one blue shark in the group begins to attack a shoal of fish, the others quickly follow, in the typical shark 'feeding frenzy'.

SPECIAL FEATURES

SHAPE: Its cone-shaped nose and streamlined body mean that the blue shark can swim thousands of kilometres without much effort.

LONG FINS: Very long pectoral fins produce an upward force that helps the shark avoid sinking as it cruises along.

Blue shark

Scientific name: *Prionace glauca*
Shark group: Carcharhinidae
Lifespan: Probably 20-plus years
Length: 3–3.5 m, occasionally 4 m
Weight: 150 kg, rarely 250 kg
Range: Worldwide tropical to cool oceans
Status: Near threatened

'STAR FACT

The blue is the shark world's greatest traveller. It regularly swims across whole oceans such as the Pacific or Atlantic on its endless hunt for food, and also as part of its breeding cycle.

DINNER TIME...

Blue sharks form a pack as they circle a shoal of small fish, such as these anchovies, driving them into a tight 'bait ball'. Then the sharks dash in one by one to eat their prey.

SKIN: Shark skin has thousands of tiny pointed 'teeth' called placoid scales or denticles. These allow water to slip past very smoothly, making swimming easier.

VISION: Most sharks have reasonable eyesight for close objects, and the blue shark's large, dark eyes are good for distance vision too.

Most animals never know that a great white is approaching until the world's biggest hunting fish crashes into them. Also known as the white pointer, blue pointer or simply 'man-eater', this predator usually surges up at its prey from dim water below and makes one fast, smash-and-grab bite. Then it backs off to taste the bits of flesh and blood in its mouth, and waits for its victim to weaken. If the shark likes its first mouthful, then it really gets to work, tearing off great chunks to swallow.

WHITE DEATH

SLICE...

The great white bite has awesome power, much greater even than that of wolves. It slices easily through gristle and even bone.

SPECIAL FEATURES

WARM BLOOD: This shark can raise its body temperature 10°C above the surrounding water, allowing it to swim faster than other, colder fish.

JAWS: Like all sharks, a great white's skeleton is made of flexible cartilage, not bone. So its jaws can bend to soak up the sudden impact of its attack.

CHARGE...

As this great white clamps its jaws onto a seal, the power of its rapid attack causes it to leap clear of the water and 'low-fly' for several metres.

Great white shark

Scientific name: *Carcharodon carcharias*
Shark group: Lamnidae
Lifespan: 20–30 years, rarely 50-plus
Length: Up to 7 m (females larger)
Weight: Up to 2 tonnes
Range: All warm and temperate seas
Status: Endangered

'STAR FACT

The great white 'spy-hops' (holds its body upright and pokes its head above the surface), presumably to look around. This is unusual among sharks but common in whales and dolphins.

TEETH: In the upper jaw, the teeth are triangular, blade-like and saw-edged for cutting. Teeth in the lower jaw are thinner and pointed for stabbing and holding.

SAW-BITE: For a big meal such as a whale, the great white bites deep and then shakes its head from side to side, to saw and cut off lumps.

The great white may be the biggest predatory fish, but the Greenland shark comes a close second. This massive monster usually lives in deep, cold water and rarely rushes anywhere. One of its favourite feasts is a 'whale fall' – a huge whale that has died and sunk to the sea bed. The Greenland shark will spend days biting and gnawing meat from the rotting carcass. When it has finally eaten its fill, it will be half as heavy again as when it arrived.

SCARY SCAVENGER

ZZZZZZ...

The Greenland shark is also called the sleeper shark because it moves so slowly and will sometimes hang motionless in the water, as though it has gone to sleep.

SPECIAL FEATURES

SPEED: Although it usually swims slowly, the Greenland shark can swish its huge tail for a burst of speed if needed, such as when hunting salmon.

SENSES: Parasites living inside the eyes of some Greenland sharks cause blindness, but the sharks can still use their senses of smell and touch to find food.

Greenland shark

Scientific name: *Somniosus microcephalus*

Shark group: Somniosidael

Lifespan: Unknown, possibly 100 years

Length: Up to 7 m (female larger)

Weight: Rarely over 1.2 tonnes

Range: Atlantic and Arctic oceans

Status: Near threatened

HI THERE...

This Greenland shark has swum into the shallow, lighter water of a river estuary. Lucky divers who spot it can get better photographs here than in the dark deep.

STAR FACT

The stomach contents of dead Greenland sharks show that they eat other sharks, salmon, many kinds of whales and dolphins, caribou (reindeer), and once even a polar bear!

DEEP DIVING: This shark can dive down to 2000 m or more, where few other big fish go, to feed on sunken dead bodies of all kinds.

TEETH: The 100 or so teeth are quite small, suited to a wide range of foods. They are narrow in the upper jaw and wide in the lower one.

Only one kind of shark swims into the freshwater of lakes and rivers, and that's the bull shark. It is bulky, muscular and mean, and doesn't mind swimming in water as shallow as one metre. It is also highly territorial, chasing away other animals that enter its home turf. That's why this tough customer is one of three shark species (kinds) known as the 'Big Three', along with the great white and tiger shark. Between them they are responsible for most of the shark attacks on humans.

FRESHLY KILLED

HUNGRY...

The bull shark will take a bite out of almost any creature, from smaller animals such as seabirds and turtles, to other sharks and even humans.

SPECIAL FEATURES

FEMALE SIZE: A female bull shark can be twice as long and three times heavier than a male. He must be wary – she could eat him!

HABITAT: Although they can swim in freshwater, thanks to some unusual body features, bull sharks are thought to return to saltwater to breed.

Bull shark

Scientific name: *Carcharhinus leucas*
Shark group: Carcharhinidae
Lifespan: 20–25 years
Length: Male 2.5 m, female 4 m
Weight: Male 120 kg, female 300 kg
Range: Warm coastal waters, rivers and lakes
Status: Near threatened

LET'S BE FRIENDS...

In the late summer bull sharks gather in groups to breed. For the rest of the year they prowl alone, although sometimes two of them form a 'friendship' and hunt together.

'STAR FACT

Bull shark attacks on humans have been recorded at locations more than 2000 km from the ocean. They have been known to bite people who have come to a riverbank to wash their clothes or swim.

AGGRESSION: Bull sharks are unpredictable – peaceful one moment, then aggressive and dangerous the next. As a result, few other animals trouble them.

BUMPING: Before racing in to bite, a bull shark will often nudge or bump a potential victim with its nose, to see how it reacts.

Not all sharks are huge, bloodthirsty predators. Some are fairly small – but they can still be deadly. Many are known as dogfish or houndfish, as they hunt shoals of fish in packs. They have two dorsal (back) fins, each with a sharp spur (spine) at the front, so they are also known as spurdogs. The spines are sharp, and can inject venom into an attacker. The poison causes a painful throbbing ache in humans and also in the shark's predators, which quickly learn to leave it alone.

SNEAK ATTACK

Spiny dogfish

Scientific name: Squalus acanthias
Shark group: Squalidae
Lifespan: 35-plus years
Length: Up to 1 m
Weight: Up to 7 kg
Range: Cool to temperate Pacific and western Atlantic oceans
Status: Vulnerable

'STAR FACT

Few other sharks have as many common names as the spiny dogfish – spiked dogfish, spiny spurdog, piked dogfish, common spurdog, piked spurshark, cape shark and cape dogfish are just a few!

LURK...

Dogfish lurk close to the sea bed, watching for any kind of prey from small fish to crabs, shellfish, prawns and even sea anemones.

SPECIAL FEATURES

COUNTER-SHADING: As in many other species, the shark's dark back blends with the sea bed, while its pale belly matches the lighter water above.

BABIES: Female spiny dogfish are pregnant for the same amount of time as female elephants. Pups are born 22 months after they start to develop.

FLAT FISH

The angel shark lies quite still on the sea bed. It has flicked sand and pebbles over itself to hide the outline of its wide, flat body, so it merges almost perfectly with its surroundings. It watches and waits until it senses a suitable fish swimming past just above. Then with frightening speed the angel shark lurches up and grabs the victim with its many small, sharp teeth. It is an ambush predator – long periods of waiting, then sudden deadly action.

HIDE...

The angel shark tries to bury itself so that only its nostrils, eyes and the breathing openings near them (the spiracles) are exposed.

Pacific angel shark

Scientific name: *Squatina californica*
Shark group: Squatinidae
Lifespan: Unknown, probably 20 years
Length: Up to 1.5 m
Weight: Up to 30 kg
Range: Pacific coasts of the Americas
Status: Near threatened

'STAR' FACT

This shark's side fins (two pectorals and two pelvics), are very flat and stick out sideways. They look almost like the wings of an aircraft – or of an angel, giving the shark its common name.

SPECIAL FEATURES

WIDE MOUTH: The strong mouth can protrude (extend forwards), stretching to form a wide tube for grabbing prey.

TRAP-JAWS: As the angel shark's mouth encloses the meal, its upper and lower jaws flick shut over it like a spring-loaded trap.

No other fish could be mistaken for the hammerhead shark. Of the nine species, most common is the scalloped hammerhead, named for the scalloped (wave-shaped) front edge of its strange head. It is not known why the eyes and nostrils are set so far apart on the hammer 'lobes', but it may increase the shark's sensitivity to smells floating through the water. Wide-set nostrils mean a smell would be much stronger in one nostril than the other, enabling the hammerhead to locate the source of the smell more quickly.

SUPER SENSITIVE

EYE SPY...

The position of their eyes, out on the ends of the head lobes, gives hammerheads a wider field of view than other sharks, which may help them locate prey faster.

SPECIAL FEATURES

SWINGING: As it swims, the hammerhead swings its head from side to side, perhaps to detect electric signals from animals in the mud.

LATERAL LINE: All sharks have a row of sensors along the side of the body – the lateral line. It detects movement in the water made by other animals.

'STAR FACT

Hammerheads regularly hunt stingrays, which hide in mud and sand on the sea bed. They even swallow the ray's hard, dagger-like tail sting. The poison does not seem to affect them.

Scalloped hammerhead shark

Scientific name: *Sphyrna lewini*
Shark group: Sphyrnidae
Lifespan: Unclear, possibly 30 years
Length: 4 m
Weight: 150 kg
Range: Coastal warm to tropical oceans
Status: Endangered

GETTING TOGETHER...

Thousands of hammerheads gather in vast shoals to find partners at breeding time.

HEAD 'WING': Its head is shaped rather like the wing of an aircraft, giving a lifting force as the hammerhead swims, which helps it to avoid sinking.

MOUTH: This shark's mouth is quite small compared to its body size because it specializes in eating fish and squid rather than really big victims.

Named for its yellow-brown upper side and much paler, yellow-tinged underside, the lemon shark is a medium-sized bottom feeder. It eats many kinds of fish, including rays, but it also gobbles up crustaceans such as crabs and crayfish, and even the occasional seabird. Lemon sharks may attack people who come too close, but there are no known human deaths. Sadly it is caught in large numbers and has become less common in recent years.

YELLOW BELLY

GIVING BIRTH...

The mother lemon shark gives birth to between five and 15 babies among the tangled roots of mangrove trees along the shore. The youngsters are about 60 cm in length.

SPECIAL FEATURES

SURVIVAL: Compared to most sharks, lemon sharks survive well in captivity. Studying them helps us to find out more about sharks in general.

LEARNING: Experiments with captive lemon sharks show that they learn quickly and remember tricks even after a gap of six months.

Lemon shark

Scientific name: *Negaprion brevirostris*
Shark group: Carcharhinidae
Lifespan: Unknown, possibly 25 years
Length: 3 m
Weight: 150 kg
Range: Coastal Atlantic and eastern Pacific oceans
Status: Near threatened

'STAR FACT

Lemon sharks are among the most saleable of sharks. People eat the flesh, boil the fins into soup, and make the skin into leather goods. They are not rare yet – but they soon could be.

LET'S GO...

Lemon sharks hang around inshore bays, harbours and estuaries during the night, then set off to hunt in deeper offshore waters by day.

DORSAL FINS: The lemon shark has two dorsal fins. The first is typically tall and shark-like but the second is unusually small and far back, just in front of the tail.

TEETH: Its smallish teeth are narrow, sharp and slightly curved, ideal for holding slippery, struggling prey such as fish and squid.

Leopards are spotty, fierce feline predators on land – and leopard sharks are the underwater version. These medium-sized carpet sharks laze around by day, resting on the sea floor, and rarely move unless threatened by a bigger shark. But at night they sneak into action and cruise slowly just above the reef, searching for prey such as smaller fish, squid and shellfish. The leopard shark's tail fin is almost as long as its body and useful for sudden bursts of speed.

WELL SPOTTED!

'STAR 'FACT

Some sharks have spiracles (extra breathing holes just behind the eyes). In the leopard shark the spiracles can be even bigger than the eyes, giving it the nickname 'four-eyed shark'.

SPECIAL FEATURES

SMELL: As in all sharks, scent particles in water float into the leopard shark's nostril chambers where micro-detectors sense them.

EYES: Sharks have an eyelid-like part called the nictitating membrane. This can move over the eye to protect it.

DOTTY...

Each leopard shark has its own pattern of patches and spots, which are different from every other leopard shark.

Leopard shark

Scientific name: *Stegostoma fasciatum*
Shark group: Orectolobiformes
Lifespan: Unknown, possibly 20–25 years
Length: 3 m
Weight: 250 kg
Range: Indian and western Pacific oceans
Status: Vulnerable

GROWING UP...

Baby leopard sharks look very different from adults. They have stripes and are known as zebra sharks.

PECTORAL FIN: The broad side or pectoral fin is used mainly for steering from side to side and going up and down, rather than for pushing the shark along.

PATTERN: No one quite knows why leopard sharks have such clear markings. It could be for camouflage, or it may help them to recognize one another.

24

A mysterious giant of the deep, dark ocean, the megamouth was not discovered until 1976. Only one or two are seen each year, so this species may be very rare – but then, the ocean is so huge that we have no way of knowing. Like whale and basking sharks, the megamouth is a filter-feeder. The brush-like gill rakers on the sides of its head sieve tiny shrimps, fish, jellyfish and other small creatures from the sea water.

BIG MOUTH

HELLO...

Megamouths are very difficult to photograph because they usually live far below the surface, where the sea is very dark. Only about 50 have ever been seen.

SPECIAL FEATURES

NOSE: The megamouth's nose is very short, with the mouth almost at its tip, rather than being low under the head as in most other sharks.

TEETH: There are hundreds of small hooked teeth, in up to 50 rows in the upper jaw and 75 in the lower. They are not needed for feeding.

Megamouth shark

Scientific name: *Megachasma pelagios*
Shark group: Megachasmidae
Lifespan: Unknown, possibly 100 years
Length: 5.5 m
Weight: Up to 1.2 tonnes
Range: Oceans worldwide
Status: Not enough information

'STAR FACT

Circular scars on the bodies of sharks such as megamouths are the result of wounds made by cookiecutter sharks. These sharp-toothed sharks feed on chunks of flesh bitten from bigger fish.

In some megamouths, the big, bendy, rubbery lips seem to glow in the dark. This is due to tiny light-producing organs called photophores.

LIGHTING UP...

BODY: Its massive body is quite soft, tubby and flabby, and the skin is loose and dark in colour. The megamouth is not a very fast swimmer.

TAIL: The upper part (lobe) of the megamouth's tail is much longer than the lower part, in a manner similar to that of another species – the thresher shark.

The sand tiger shark's many common names include rag-tooth, snaggle-tooth and thin-tooth, as its teeth are very spiky and wide-set. It is a fearsome hunter of small fish such as herring, mackerel, flatfish and also baby sharks. The sand tiger does not mind chasing food into the shallows. This fearsome fish will even wriggle right up to where the waves lap on the beach, before turning round and splashing back into deeper water.

SNAGGLE-TOOTH

PROWL...

By day, sand tigers laze around in caves or rocky cracks. At night they come out to hunt in packs, herding fish into 'bait balls'.

'STAR 'FACT

The sand tiger shark swallows air to alter its buoyancy (ability to float). More air inside its body makes the shark lighter, so it can stay near the surface. It then belches out the air to sink. This saves swimming energy.

SPECIAL FEATURES

TAIL: Sharks swim by swishing their tails from side to side. Although the sand tiger is a bulky, sluggish shark it can make sudden fast dashes.

REAR FINS: The two lower rear side fins, called the pelvics, help the sand tiger shark to turn sharply to the left or right.

The sand tiger has about three rows of teeth with up to 50 teeth in its upper jaw, and the same in its lower jaw.

SMILE...

Sand tiger shark

Scientific name: Carcharias taurus
Shark group: Carcharhinidae
Lifespan: 15–20 years
Length: 3 m
Weight: 150 kg
Range: Warm to tropical oceans
Status: Vulnerable

GILL SLITS: Like other sharks, the sand tiger takes in oxygen by passing water over its gills. Unusually, its gill slits are in front of its pectoral fins, and are very low.

SNOUT: Also called the grey nurse shark, the sand tiger has a streamlined narrow snout, with the mouth set some way back, below the eyes.

The whitetip reef shark spends its nights poking its nose into all kinds of cracks, crevices, holes and caves on the reef. It is looking for any prey that has tried to hide, from fish to lobsters, crabs and even octopus. Most sharks have tough skin, and the whitetip's is thick and extra-strong, to prevent scrapes and cuts as it squeezes past jagged rocks and sharp corals.

SLIM WRIGGLER

Whitetip reef shark

Scientific name: *Triaenodon obesuss*
Shark group: Carcharhinidae
Lifespan: 20-plus years
Length: Up to 2 m
Weight: Up to 20 kg
Range: Tropical and subtropical Indian and Pacific oceans
Status: Near threatened

AFTER YOU...

In the breeding season, whitetip reef sharks gather in shallow water to choose their partners, the males following the females.

STAR FACT

Some sharks are territorial, with a favourite place that they defend from intruders. Whitetip reef sharks have regular resting places that they may use over many years.

SPECIAL FEATURES

FIN TIPS: The whitetip is named after the pale tips on its front dorsal (back) fin and the upper end of its tail fin.

FLEXIBLE BODY: Very bendy fins and a slim, supple body allow the whitetip to squirm into very narrow gaps around the reef.

Like many sharks, the bamboo shark is nocturnal – a night-time hunter. Like other sharks too, its camouflaging pattern tends to fade as it gets older and bigger, because fewer predators will try to attack bigger prey. Under cover of darkness on the coral reef, this slow swimmer spends its time sneaking up on many kinds of crabs, shrimps and worms, and then grabbing them with a sudden dash and bite.

SHADY SWIMMER

SQUIRT...

Bamboo sharks have been seen squirting water at small fish hiding in rocky cracks, trying to swish them out so they can eat them.

'STAR FACT

The bamboo shark is popular in aquariums because it doesn't get too big and will eat a wide range of food. Many shark species refuse food in captivity, and starve to death.

Bamboo shark

Scientific name: *Chiloscyllium punctatum*
Shark group: Hemiscylliidae
Lifespan: Unknown, possibly 15–20 years
Length: 1 m
Weight: 15 kg
Range: Southeast Asian and western Pacific coasts
Status: Near threatened

SPECIAL FEATURES

BODY BANDS: Its horizontal bands help the young bamboo shark to merge into the shadows and moonlit patches on the reef at night.

BARBELS: Two long, thin feelers above the mouth, called barbels, help the shark feel its way by touch even in complete darkness.

The Port Jackson shark disproves the popular belief that sharks must keep swimming to stay alive. All sharks need water passing over their gills to bring continuing supplies of life-giving oxygen. But the Port Jackson shark can do this while lazing on the sea bed. The muscles in its mouth and chin make pumping movements, sucking water in through the mouth and pushing it out over the gills. Often lots of these sharks will lie in a pile on the sea bed.

SANDY SNOOZER

OUCH...

Each of its dorsal or back fins has a sharp spine at its front end, which makes the Port Jackson shark difficult for predators to swallow.

STAR FACT

If the Port Jackson shark eats something its body is unable to digest, it can turn its stomach inside out and spit it out of its mouth to get rid of the unwanted contents.

SPECIAL FEATURES

HEAD: The Port Jackson shark has a tall, wide head, large eyebrow ridges and a small mouth. It belongs to the group called the bullhead sharks.

SPIRACLES: As in a few other sharks, small openings called spiracles lie just behind each of this shark's eyes, helping the water flow for breathing.

Port Jackson shark

Scientific name: *Heterodontus portusjacksoni*
Shark group: Heterodontidae
Lifespan: Unknown, perhaps 30 years
Length: Up to 1.5 m
Weight: 15–20 kg
Range: Australian coasts
Status: Least concern

KEEPING SAFE...

The egg cases of the Port Jackson shark have a strange corkscrew shape. This helps the eggs stay safely hidden in mud and weeds until they hatch.

FRONT TEETH: Its small, sharp front teeth are perfect for pulling little shellfish, crabs, shrimps and worms from the sea bed.

BACK TEETH: This shark's large, flat, slab-like back teeth are ideal for crushing and chewing hard-shelled foods such as mussels and clams.

Also called the puffer shark or balloon shark, the swell shark's special trick is to blow itself up! If threatened, this shark gulps water into the front part of its stomach, in the middle of its body. Doing this makes its body expand, causing it to become twice as fat as usual. It also curls itself right around and holds its tail in its mouth. It is then too big and awkward for most predators to eat. The swell shark can blow up very quickly, but it takes a while to return to its normal size.

BLOWN UP!

'STAR FACT

If the swell shark is near the surface it can gulp in air to make itself swell up. When the danger is past and the shark lets out the air, it makes a barking or yapping noise, almost like a dog!

HIDE...

This shark's spots and patches provide excellent camouflage, blending with the stony sea bed, especially at night when the water is very dark.

SPECIAL FEATURES

BIG EYES: Its large, cat-like eyes have upright pupils to let in plenty of light, as the swell shark is a nocturnal hunter.

HUGE MOUTH: Almost no other shark has such a wide, huge mouth compared to its body size – not even the great white!

Swell shark

Scientific name: *Cephaloscyllium ventriosum*

Shark group: Scyliorhinidae

Lifespan: Unknown, possibly 20–30 years

Length: 1 m

Weight: 25 kg

Range: North American Pacific coasts

Status: Least concern

MERMAID'S PURSES...

Like many sharks, swell shark eggs have tough cases, called mermaid's purses. Their twirly strings hold them in the seaweed, where egg-eating animals are less likely to spot them.

SUCTION GULP: As well as lots of small sharp teeth to grab victims, the swell shark can also open its big mouth wide with sudden power to suck them in.

DENS: Each swell shark has favourite caves and cracks to rest in by day. If a predator tries to get it out, the shark swells up, becoming impossible to remove.

Big, heavy, and strong, with a mouth full of extremely sharp teeth – plus a massive appetite – few other marine creatures would tangle with a tiger shark. Without warning it will suddenly charge with lightning speed and bite hard. This makes it one of the 'Big Three' most dangerous sharks to humans, along with the great white and the bull shark. This formidable predator eats anything it can swallow – big or small, alive or dead. It is even known to be a cannibal, which means that it eats others of its own kind.

TIGER OF THE SEA

HITCHING A RIDE...

Remoras, also known as sharksucker fish, hitch rides on sharks! Using their suction fins, they attach themselves to the shark's body and get carried along. They do little lasting damage to the shark.

SPECIAL FEATURES

STRIPES: Tiger sharks are named for their markings. Their upright dark and pale stripes split and merge, just like those of real tigers.

CAMOUFLAGE: Young tiger sharks have dark stripes for camouflage in seaweed. The stripes fade as they mature and swim into the open ocean.

SHINE...

Sharks such as the tiger shark have a shiny reflecting layer inside the eye to catch more light, helping them to see better in gloomy night-time waters.

Tiger shark

Scientific name: *Galeocerdo cuvier*
Shark group: Carcharhinidae
Lifespan: 25-plus years
Length: 4.5 m (female larger)
Weight: Up to 650 kg
Range: Tropical and warm oceans
Status: Near threatened

'STAR FACT

Tiger sharks will not only swallow almost any food. They also gulp down inedible objects such as tyres, bottles, lumps of wood and plastic, clothes, and even a musical drum.

DORSAL PIVOT: As well as helping the shark to swim straight, the dorsal (back) fin works as a pivot or swivel, which the shark swings around to change direction fast.

LIFTING FINS: Sharks tend to sink slowly as they swim, but angling the pectoral (front side) fins upwards slightly gives a lifting force to keep the nose up.

The biggest fish in the sea is also one of the most peaceful. The whale shark is larger than some types of whales, and so huge and powerful that it has little to fear – but only once it is grown up. As a baby, it's just 30–50 centimetres in length, and makes a tasty mouthful for many other kinds of sharks. Like the basking and megamouth sharks, the whale shark is a filter-feeder. Its frilly gill rakers strain small animals such as krill and baby fish from the water.

PEACEFUL GIANT

CAREFUL...

Whale sharks usually swim slowly when people are around. The main risk to human swimmers is a knock from the shark's enormous tail if it is suddenly frightened.

'STAR FACT

Whale sharks do not fear divers, and don't mind boats, unless these get too close. In fact these sharks seem to enjoy 'playing' as they twist, turn and give rides to human swimmers who pay them a visit.

SPECIAL FEATURES

MARKINGS: Each whale shark has its own pattern of spots, blotches and stripes that seem to change colour as the sun changes its angle.

RIDGES: Three raised ridges (keels) run along each side of the body. It is possible that they help water flow past the shark's body more smoothly.

Whale shark

Scientific name: *Rhincodon typus*
Shark group: Rhincodontidae
Lifespan: 70-plus years
Length: Up to 12 m
Weight: Up to 12.5 tonnes
Range: Tropical and warm oceans
Status: Vulnerable

WATCH OUT...

Whale sharks feed mainly on very small food items, little bigger than your fingers. But recent studies show they will surge at a shoal of bigger fish, open wide and gulp them in.

FEEDING: To feed without swimming, the shark sucks in water, closes its mouth and pushes the water out through its gill slits, trapping food on the rakers.

TEETH: The whale shark has hundreds of tiny teeth along its jaws, but these are not used for feeding – or for anything else, as far as we know.

It might seem like a lovely life, lazing around on the sea bed in the warm tropical shallows. This is how the wobbegong or 'wobby' goes hunting. It lies quite still, allowing its amazing camouflage to do all the work. Multicoloured flaps of skin, floppy frills and tassels hang from the wobbegong's head and body, disguising its outline so that it blends beautifully with the rocks and weeds around it. If a careless sea creature happens to swim close, the wobby leaps into action and gulps it straight down.

LAZY LIFE

OPEN WIDE...

A front view shows the wobbegong's wide mouth, frilly barbels (feelers), and the sharp, gappy teeth that ensure victims do not struggle free.

SPECIAL FEATURES

CAUDAL FIN: The lower part of the wobbegong's caudal (tail) fin is very small, so it can lie as flat as possible on the sea bed.

CAMOUFLAGE: When hunting, the wobby tries to find a patch of sea bed with the same colours as its own body, for the best camouflage.

Spotted wobbegong

Scientific name: *Orectolobus maculatus*
Shark group: Orectolobidae
Lifespan: Unknown, possibly 30-plus years
Length: Up to 3 m
Weight: Up to 100 kg
Range: Eastern Indian Ocean, around Australia
Status: Near threatened

'STAR FACT

Wobbegongs have been spotted wriggling and hauling themselves across seashore rocks to get back into the ocean, usually after being trapped in a rock pool by the falling tide.

KEEP LOW...

The wobbegong is a member of the carpet shark group. Its body is flattened from the top to underside, so it lies better on the sea bed.

SUCKING POWER: The wobbegong opens its mouth wide with such power that water is sucked in with great force – carrying nearby prey along with it.

WHISKERS: Small string-like barbels and tassels hang around the wobby's mouth and wave in the current, attracting curious creatures for lunch.

Few other sea creatures can escape a shortfin mako when this shark is swimming at full speed. Smooth and super-streamlined, it dashes after tuna, bluefish and even swordfish, which are themselves among the champion speedy swimmers. The mako can also twist and swerve faster than the human eye can follow. Once its sharp, curved teeth jab into flesh and its jaws get a good grip, the quarry is dead meat.

RAPID STRIKE

Shortfin mako

Scientific name: Isurus oxyrinchus
Shark group: Lamnidae
Lifespan: Unclear, perhaps 20–25 years
Length: Usually up to 3 m
Weight: Varies widely, 150–400 kg
Range: Tropical to cool oceans
Status: Vulnerable

'STAR FACT

There's no quicker shark than the shortfin mako. It can race along in sudden short bursts at more than 70 km/h. This puts it among the top ten fastest fish in the sea.

WOW...

Sharks have tiny ampullae (pits) on their head and snouts. These detect natural electrical pulses given off by the muscles of other animals.

SPECIAL FEATURES

TEETH: Sharks grow new teeth continually at the back of the jaw. These move forwards slowly for use. This mako has three rows of working teeth.

LEAPING: The mako can escape danger, such as a bigger shark, by leaping clear of the water – as high as 7 m above the surface.